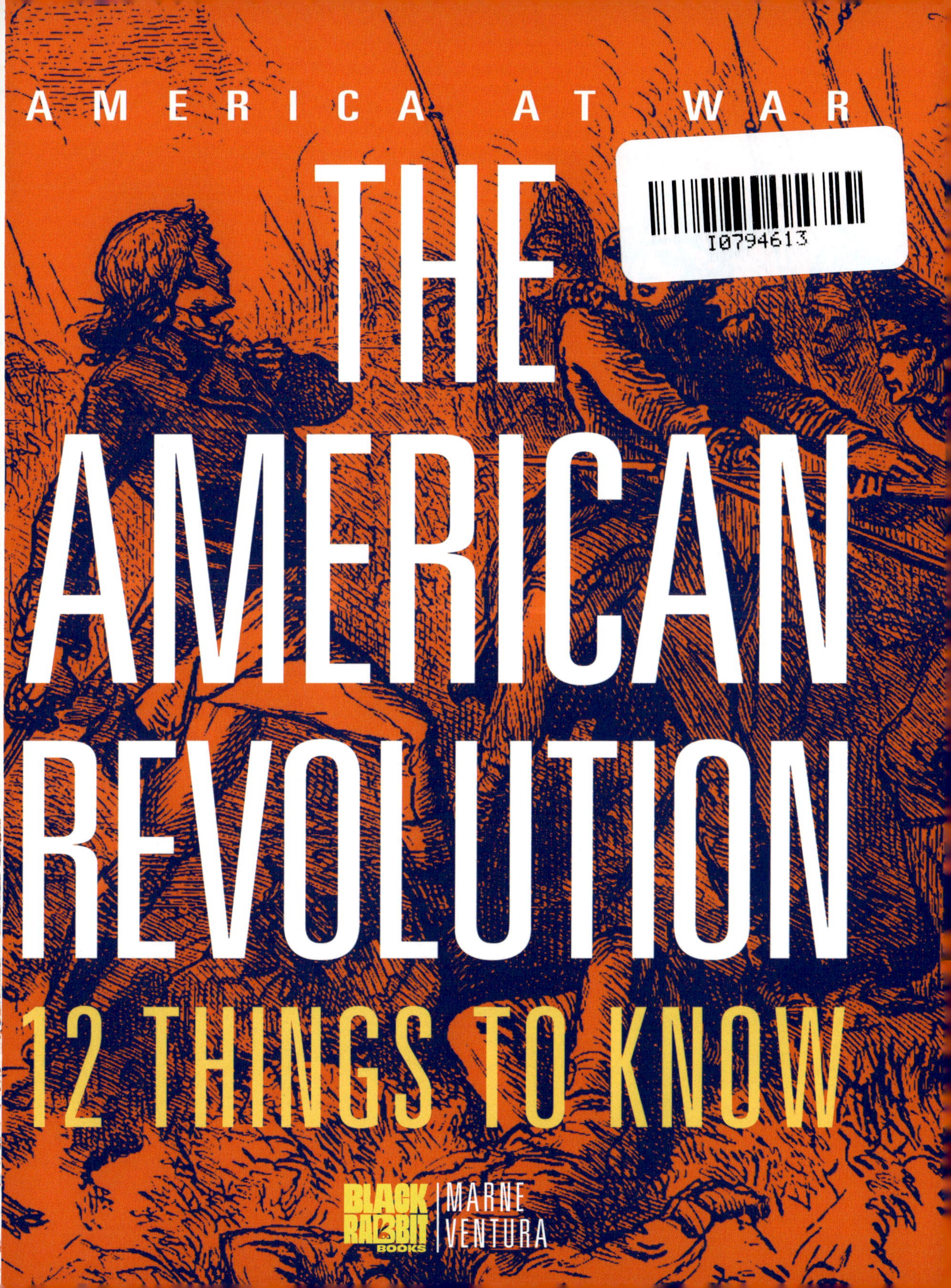

AMERICA AT WAR

THE AMERICAN REVOLUTION

12 THINGS TO KNOW

BLACK RABBIT BOOKS

MARNE VENTURA

Table of Contents

Repeal of the
Stamp Act, 1766
FOREVER/USA
2016

Great Britain Places Unfair Taxes *on Colonists*

1

Starting in the 1600s, Great Britain ruled the American colonies. France ruled the colonies to the west of this region. The British and the French fought to get more land. This was the French and Indian War (1754–63).

After the war, the British needed money for their army. They added **taxes** to the American colonists to raise funds. The Stamp Act was passed on March 22, 1765. It taxed all printed materials. Agents stamped the items to show the tax was paid. The colonists did not like this. They thought the tax was unfair. But they had no voice in British government.

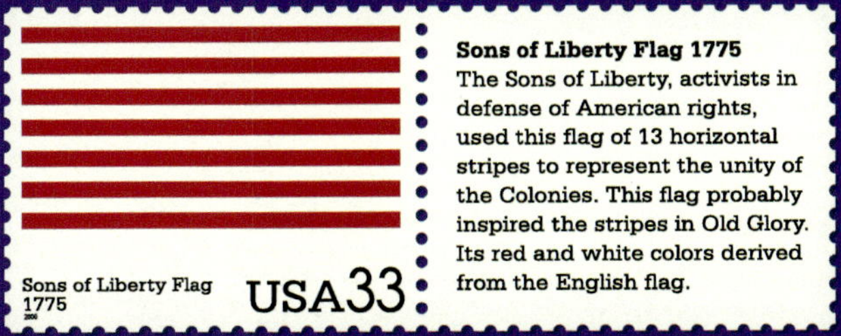

Many colonists called for a boycott on British goods. One group was called the Sons of Liberty. They went after British stamp agents. They destroyed stamps and records. They attacked people who did not follow the boycott. The British government **repealed** the act. But it was not their last act against the colonies.

Great Britain passed the Tea Act in 1773. This gave the British-owned East India Company an unfair edge on tea sales. East India Company paid no taxes to sell tea. But the colonists were still taxed when buying the tea. This made them unhappy. They were tired of the British government making decisions for them. They wanted to have a voice in the government.

Tea was a common drink, making the tea tax very unpopular.

BOYCOTT A boycott is a refusal to buy or use a product. People may boycott a business or a person. They might even boycott goods from a country. Its purpose is to speak out and bring about a change. The word comes from an Irish landlord. His name was Boycott (1832–97). He treated his renters poorly. Eventually, no one would work for him. They would not sell him food or even deliver his mail.

New York colonists react angrily to the announcement of the Tea Act.

13 Number of American colonies ruled by Great Britain.

The Stamp Act taxed newspapers, pamphlets, wills, and playing cards. • The East India Company's tea cost less than anyone else's. • But buying it supported the Tea Act.

2 Colonists Protest with *Boston Tea Party*

In 1773, the East India Company loaded its ships with tea. They set out for the colonies. The Sons of Liberty tried to keep the ships from docking. The ships meant for Philadelphia and New York turned back. But three ships were able to land in Boston. The first one was the *Dartmouth*. It docked in late November. British law said cargo had to be unloaded within 20 days.

On November 29, Samuel Adams called for a meeting. Thousands of people showed up. They assigned men to watch the ship. They made sure no tea was unloaded. The ship couldn't leave either.

The *Dartmouth's* 20-day docking period was up on December 16. That night, the Sons of Liberty took charge. They dressed as members of the Mohawk tribe. Encouraged by the large crowd, they boarded the

92,586 Weight in pounds (41,996 kilograms) of tea dumped into Boston Harbor.

Colonists bought about 1.2 million pounds (544,310 kg) of tea each year. • All the dumped tea would be worth about $1.7 million today. • The tea in the water caused a terrible smell.

Tea chests were hacked open with tomahawks and axes.

ships. They were armed with axes. They smashed 342 tea chests. Then they dumped the tea into the ocean.

Around 60 men boarded the ships. But thousands of people watched from the shore. This night was one of the first major acts of rebellion against the British. The dumped tea was an expensive loss. The harbor was shut down until the colonists paid for it.

THINK ABOUT IT Were the Sons of Liberty right to dump the tea into Boston Harbor? Why or why not? Was there another way they could have protested the taxes?

A chest of tea weighed 400 pounds (181 kg).

Congress Appeals to *King George III*

3

British rulers wanted to punish the colonists for the Boston Tea Party. In 1774, they passed four new laws. In Britain, they were called the **Coercive** Acts. But in the colonies, they were known as the Intolerable Acts.

The first act closed Boston Harbor. The next act severely limited the ability to hold town meetings. Colonists needed British approval first. The act also gave Great Britain the right to choose all colonial officials. A third act protected British officials against crimes in the colony. These first three acts only applied to the Massachusetts colony. The final act applied to all of the colonies. It forced colonists to give housing and food to British soldiers.

The new acts angered the colonists further. They felt the acts took away their rights. They fought them.

King George III

The First Continental Congress was formed. It met in Philadelphia, Pennsylvania. The meeting began on September 5, 1774. Twelve colonies sent people to represent them. Georgia did not send anyone. The colony still needed British help to battle Indigenous people.

On October 20, the **delegates** approved the Articles of Association. It was a warning to Great Britain. The colonies wanted the Intolerable Acts to end. If not, a boycott of all British goods would begin. All **exports** to Great Britain would also stop. The Congress also sent a letter to King George III. It asked for the acts to be repealed. The colonies also wanted self-government.

56 Number of delegates sent to the First Continental Congress.

At first, the delegates did not trust each other.
- Some wanted to settle with Great Britain. Others wanted to declare independence from British rule.
- They met in secret for two months.

Delegates discuss how to respond to British ill treatment.

Paul Revere Warns of *British Approach*

4

King George III ignored the letter for self-rule. This angered the colonists even more. They began to gather weapons. But a British governor in Concord, Massachusetts found out. British troops from Boston were sent to destroy the weapons. They also planned to capture colonial leaders John Hancock and Samuel Adams.

The British army's plans were discovered. A man named Paul Revere belonged to the Sons of Liberty. He often carried messages on horseback between colonial leaders. On the night of April 16, 1775, Revere rode to Concord. He told the colonists that the British were on their way. He also set up a warning system. Guards used lanterns as signals in the Old North Church in Boston. One lantern meant the British would come by land. Two meant they would come by water.

SENDING THE SIGNAL

On the night of April 18, 1775, two men entered the Old North Church. They climbed a staircase. There was a small door to the church's tower hidden behind a pipe organ. They climbed eight flights of stairs in darkness to get to the top. When they reached the top, they leaned out a window to signal with the lanterns.

700 Number of British soldiers who came to Lexington on April 18, 1775.

William Dawes and Samuel Prescott also helped warn leaders. • Paul Revere is a folk hero of the American Revolution. • His midnight ride is the subject of a famous poem by Henry Wadsworth Longfellow.

On April 18, 1775, Revere saw the flash of two lanterns. He set out to warn Adams and Hancock. The leaders were in Lexington, Massachusetts. Revere made it there in time. Hancock and Adams were able to flee. Because of Revere's warning, colonial fighters were ready for battle the next morning.

THINK ABOUT IT

How might things have been different if the British had won the Revolutionary War?

John Hancock

Samuel Adams

First Shot of American Revolution *Is Fired*

5

The people in Lexington knew the British were nearby. Some of the town's army waited for the British to arrive. They called themselves minutemen. They could be ready to fight at a minute's notice. Their captain told them, "Stand your ground. Don't fire unless fired upon. But if they want to have a war, let it begin here."

The British got to Lexington at around 5:00 a.m. The minutemen were ready. Both sides stared each other down in the town square. They were nervous. Nobody was sure what to do. Suddenly, a shot rang out. No one is sure who fired it. But it caused others to start shooting too. Eight colonists were killed. Ten more were wounded. Only one British soldier was hurt.

After that, the British army moved toward Concord. Colonial troops waited for them at the North Bridge outside of town. There were 500 minutemen. The

British troops numbered about 700. When the minutemen started firing, the British fell back. The minutemen hid behind walls, houses, and trees. They kept taking shots at the British as they left Concord.

This was not a major battle. But "the shot heard around the world" sent a message to people on both sides. The colonists proved they could stand up to the British. The American Revolution had begun.

Captain John Parker led the minutemen in Lexington. A statue of him now stands at that place.

70 Number of minutemen who met British troops in Lexington.

Colonists fighting against the British called themselves Patriots. • Colonists still loyal to Great Britain were called Loyalists. • The colonists called British troops "Redcoats." They wore red coats with brass buttons.

A painting shows the colonists firing at the British in the Battle of Lexington.

"the shot
heard around
the world"

Great Britain Wins at *Bunker Hill*

6

After the battles at Lexington and Concord, the British made a plan. They refused to be defeated again. Their plan was to take control of the hills above Boston. They had about 10,000 men ready to fight. Their leader was General Thomas Gage.

On June 16, 1775, the colonist army prepared for the attack. The 1,200 men were led by Colonel William Prescott. Their mission was to defend Bunker Hill. For reasons never made clear, Prescott changed the plan. He led his men to Breed's Hill instead. They spent all night building a 6-foot (1.8-meter) earthen wall. This would protect them from British gunfire.

The next morning, three British warships fired at Boston. Most of the shells went into the side of Breed's Hill. The British could not angle their guns high enough. Their shots did

General Thomas Gage

not reach the earthen wall at the very top. They decided to attack from the other side of the hill. Twenty-eight barges carried 1,500 Redcoats there.

The colonists held their ground. But they ran out of ammunition first. Great Britain won the battle. They took over the hill. But the British suffered many deaths. Many men were wounded. The British commander William Howe said, "The success is too dearly bought."

Colonel William Prescott (center) led the American troops in the Battle of Bunker Hill.

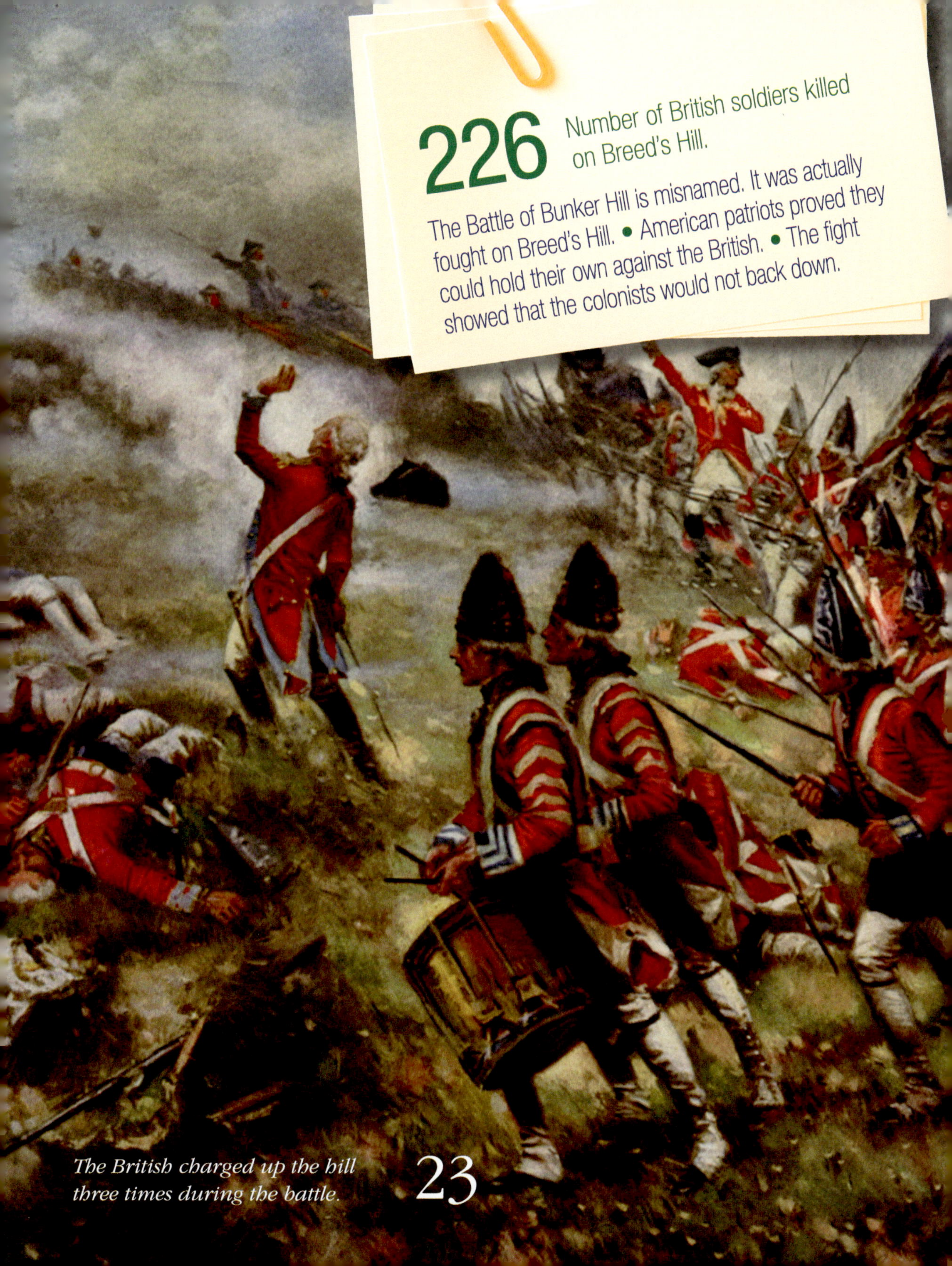

226 Number of British soldiers killed on Breed's Hill.

The Battle of Bunker Hill is misnamed. It was actually fought on Breed's Hill. • American patriots proved they could hold their own against the British. • The fight showed that the colonists would not back down.

The British charged up the hill three times during the battle.

Congress Approves the Declaration *of Independence*

7

In 1775, the Second Continental Congress met. It took place in the Pennsylvania State House. There were 65 delegates this time. All 13 colonies were represented.

The delegates talked about King George III. The king would not meet their demands. The British rulers had denied colonists the right to self-government. There was no other choice. It was time for a real fight. The colonists would raise funds to form their own Continental Army. Each state would send men to fight for one year.

Next, delegates drafted the **Declaration** of Independence. It stated the colonies were no longer under British rule. They were now a new country. They called it the United States of America. It also said all men are created equal. They have certain

500 Copies of the Declaration immediately printed and handed out.

It was mostly written by Thomas Jefferson. • Only 56 delegates signed the final copy. This copy is on display at the National Archives in Washington, DC. • Most delegates signed on August 2, 1776.

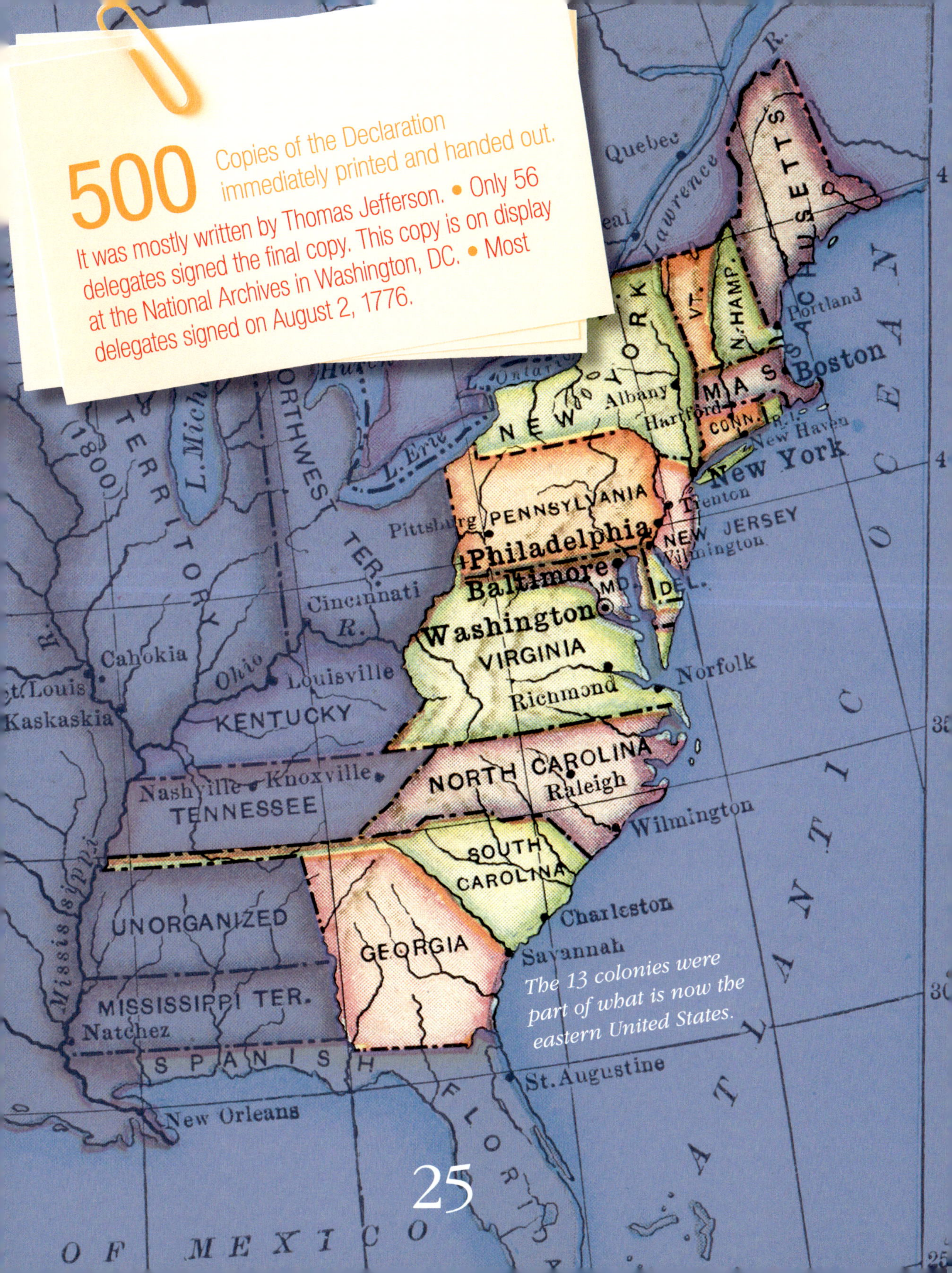

The 13 colonies were part of what is now the eastern United States.

rights. These include "life, liberty, and the pursuit of happiness."

Over the winter of 1775 to 1776, they worked on the document. It was approved on July 4, 1776. This date became the new nation's birthday. On July 8, 1776, the Liberty Bell in Philadelphia rang. It called the people together. They listened to the Declaration of Independence being read aloud.

THE LIBERTY BELL

The Liberty Bell was built in 1751. It cracked during a test. Then it was remade. The new bell broke in 1835. In 1846, the bell was rung to celebrate George Washington's birthday. The crack grew in size. It could not be fixed.

George Washington Heads *the Army*

8

The Continental Army needed a leader. Delegates at the Second Continental Congress chose George Washington. His soldiers had little or no battle experience. The new army was much smaller than the British army. But they had something bigger to fight for.

At first, the army didn't see much success. It lost several battles in 1775 and 1776. Washington knew his men needed a win. On Christmas night in 1776, he led 2,400 men across the Delaware River. They made a surprise attack in Trenton, New Jersey. Hessians were posted there. They were German soldiers hired by the British. But they had spent all night celebrating the holiday. They were fast asleep when Washington's men approached. More than 1,000 Hessians were captured.

Washington's win at Trenton was the first of many. Each victory improved the soldiers' spirits. More men joined

43 Washington's age when he became commander-in-chief of the army.

Washington was a leader in the French and Indian War. • He helped organize the troops and kept spirits high. • His success with the army led to his election as the first US president.

George Washington and his men cross the Delaware River.

the army. On October 7, 1777, the Battle of Saratoga took place in New York. The British were surrounded by 13,000 to 17,000 American troops. The Redcoats gave up. The US victory was a turning point in the war.

In 1778, France joined the colonists in their fight. The British and French were longtime **foes**. France saw a chance to gain a new **ally**. It helped the states with supplies, weapons, and money. Most importantly, France sent troops and its navy to help fight.

Think About It

Do you think the United States would still have won the war without France's help? Why or why not?

Continental Army Spends Winter *at Valley Forge*

9

The winter of 1777 to 1778 was cold and harsh. It brought hard times to the Continental Army. Washington set up camp at Valley Forge in Pennsylvania. Only 8,000 men were still fit to fight. Most only wore ragged clothing. There were no coats or blankets. Many were barefoot.

Washington chose the area for safety. The men watched for British soldiers on tree-covered hills. A river was on one side. A creek was on the other. But there were no buildings.

Washington had his men build simple log cabins. Each hut was 14-by-16 feet (4.3-by-4.9 meters). A hut held 12 men. They slept on the floor. Cold air leaked in. There was little food. There was no meat or vegetables. For two months, they lived on bread alone. It was called fire cake. It was easy to make and lasted a long time. But it was not tasty or healthy. Sickness spread through the camp.

Baron von Steuben came to the men's aid. He was a Prussian military officer. He was sent by the French. Von Steuben taught the men to be better fighters. He helped raise their spirits. By spring, the troops left Valley Forge ready to continue fighting.

Think About It Pretend you are a US soldier. You are spending the winter at Valley Forge. Write a letter to your family to describe the experience.

Snow covers the cannons at Valley Forge National Historical Park near Philadelphia.

George Washington leads the Continental Army to Valley Forge in 1777.

2,000 Number of soldiers who died during the winter at Valley Forge.

Fire cake was dough made of water and flour. It was cooked over a fire. • Valley Forge was a day's march from Philadelphia. • At the end of March, 2,898 men were not ready to fight. They did not have suitable clothing.

British Surrender *at Yorktown*

10

In late 1778, British General Charles Cornwallis moved his army to the southern states. He hoped to cut off supplies and soldiers going to Washington's army. It was also believed that more British supporters lived in the South. By May 1780, Cornwallis and his men were spread across Georgia and South Carolina.

Washington sent General Nathanael Greene to the South. Greene was to lead his troops against Cornwallis. It was a big job. So far, the Continental Army had not done well in the southern states. But Washington chose well. Greene and Cornwallis clashed in the Carolinas. Many British soldiers were killed.

Cornwallis moved his troops to Yorktown, Virginia in 1781. He planned to wait for more supplies and troops from Great Britain. While he waited, 7,000 French soldiers joined Washington near New York

City. American and French soldiers set out on the 200-mile (322-kilometer) march to Yorktown.

Meanwhile, 36 French warships kept the British navy from removing Cornwallis' army. The French ships also blocked the British navy from sending support. By October 1781, Washington's 20,000 soldiers surrounded 9,500 British troops. Cornwallis and his troops had no way to escape. Cornwallis asked for a **ceasefire** on October 17, 1781. He sent his deputy to offer his sword in surrender. The official surrender took place on October 19.

American
General Nathanael Greene

British
General Charles Cornwallis

15 Days it took Washington's army to march from New York to Yorktown.

Both armies moved south because of a standstill in the North. • Yorktown was the last major battle of the war. • The surrender led to the end of British rule in the states.

British forces surrendered after the Battle of Yorktown.

Treaty of Paris Brings End *to War*

11

The American Revolution officially ended on September 3, 1783. That day, the United States and Great Britain signed the **Treaty** of Paris.

The two countries met in France. The US Congress sent men to represent the United States. They were Benjamin Franklin, John Adams, and John Jay. Franklin had been a face for the United States in France since 1776. Adams was chosen because he stood strong against Great Britain and France. Jay was a lawyer. He was already working in Europe. His goal was to further America's success. David Hartley signed for King George III. Hartley was a member of the British **Parliament**. Both countries **ratified** the deal in 1784.

The Treaty of Paris is located in Washington, DC, today.

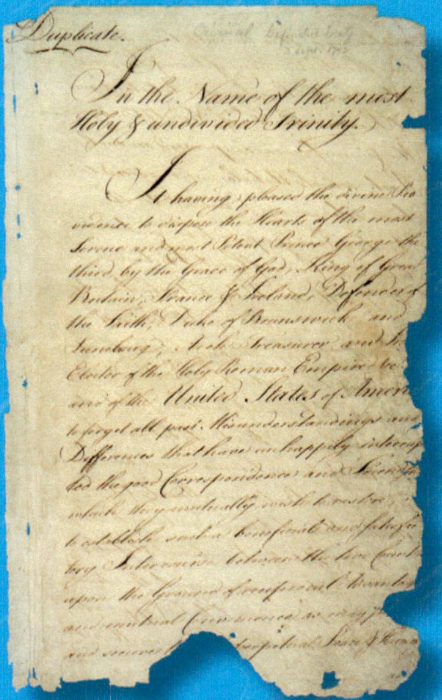

Unfinished painting of peace agreements showing the American delegates. British delegates refused to pose.

The treaty recognized the United States as its own nation. It granted the states independence from Great Britain. It also set wider boundaries for the new nation. The Mississippi River became the western border. The Great Lakes bordered the north. American fishermen were given fishing rights off the coast of Newfoundland, Canada. The United States also agreed not to punish any Loyalists. These were Americans who supported the British throughout the war. Any property taken from them was returned.

278 Number of days it took to sign the Treaty of Paris.

Formal talks to end the war began in April 1782. • The treaty was first drafted on November 30, 1782. • The treaty is named after the place where it was agreed upon and signed.

States Are United under the *US Constitution*

12

During the war, the Articles of Confederation were written. The document was an agreement by all 13 colonies. It was the nation's first **constitution**. It created a national government, but it was weak. The states held most of the power. They were still mostly separate.

After the war, some Americans sought a new constitution. They wanted stronger national government. Then the country would be more united.

In 1787, all states except Rhode Island sent delegates to Philadelphia. The goal was to create the US Constitution. This document would lay out how the government would work. All states would follow it.

The Constitution helped balance the power between state and national governments. It created checks and balances. The national government was split into three branches. Any power not assigned to a branch was given to the states to decide. The Constitution also outlined voting rights and how to elect a leader. George Washington was elected as US president. John Adams became the vice president.

The Constitution went into effect on March 9, 1789. The United States was now an independent nation. It had its own rules and its own rulers. The lives lost and the battles won had made it possible.

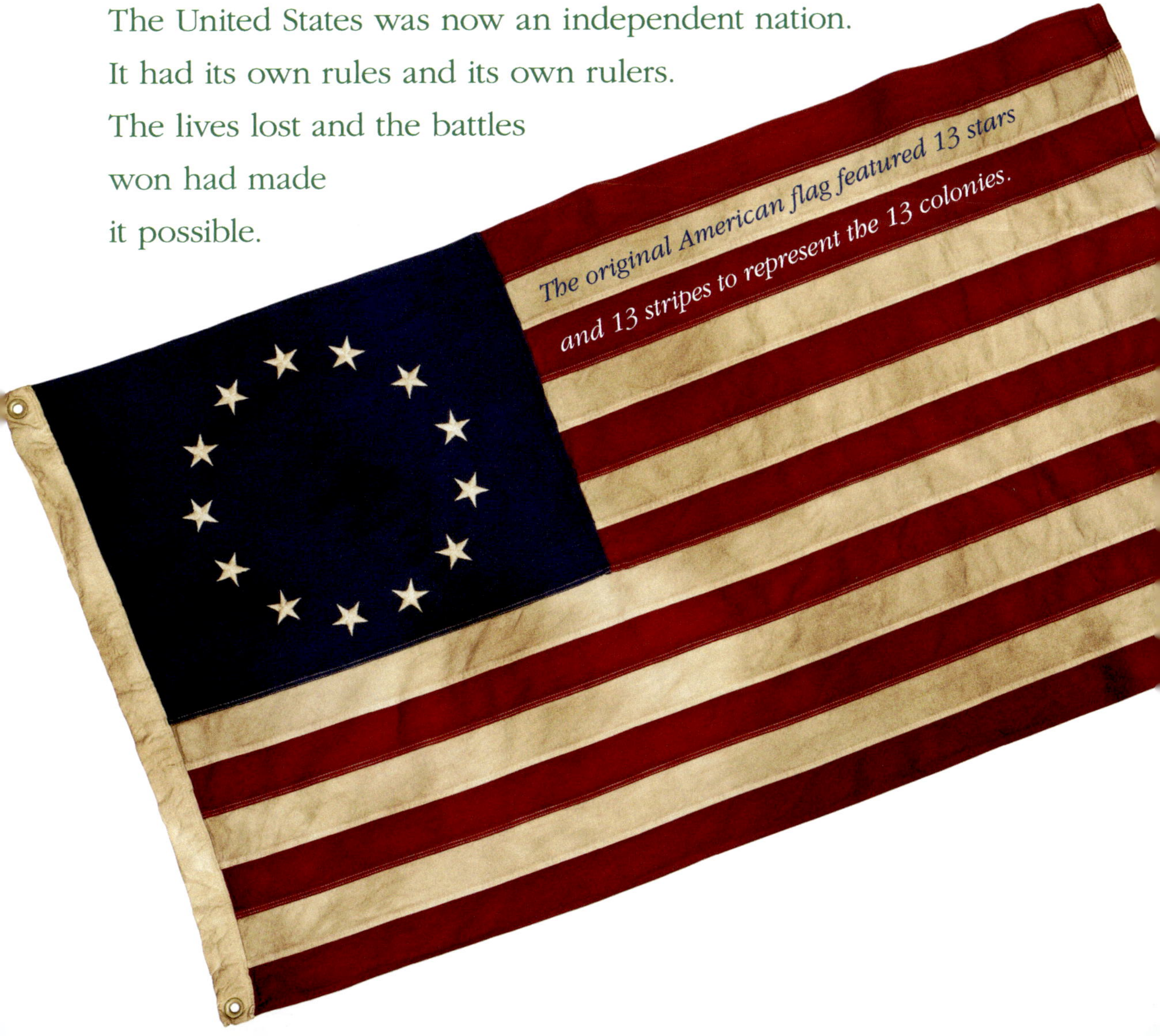

The original American flag featured 13 stars and 13 stripes to represent the 13 colonies.

8 Number of years the American Revolutionary War lasted.

The Bill of Rights was written after the Constitution was ratified. • It includes the first 10 **amendments** to the Constitution. • These are basic rights that the government cannot take away.

AMERICAN EXTREMES

Much debate was around representation in the national government. Larger states wanted a number based on population. Smaller states objected. They wanted each state to have an equal vote. A compromise was made. The House of Representatives would have delegates based on population. In the Senate, each state got two delegates total.

Today, the US Constitution has 27 amendments.

12 Key Dates

March 22, 1765
Great Britain passes the Stamp Act, the first of many taxes on the colonies.

December 16, 1773
The Sons of Liberty dump tea in Boston Harbor.

September 5, 1774
The First Continental Congress meets.

April 19, 1775
The Battles of Lexington and Concord start the American Revolution.

May 10, 1775
The Second Continental Congress meets.

June 16, 1775
Colonial and British troops clash at Breed's Hill.

March 22, 1765

December 16, 1773

April 19, 1775

July 4, 1776
The Declaration of Independence is approved.

December 25, 1776
George Washington leads troops across the Delaware River. They capture 1,000 Hessians

October 7, 1777
US troops defeat the British at the Battle of Saratoga.

October 17, 1781
British General Cornwallis surrenders at the Battle of Yorktown.

September 3, 1783
The Treaty of Paris is signed in France. The American Revolution officially ends.

May 25, 1787
The Constitutional Convention begins in Philadelphia.

July 4, 1776

September, 1783

December 25, 1776

Glossary

ally
A country that supports and helps another country in a war.

amendment
A change to a law or legal document.

ceasefire
A period of where fighting stops and usually peace talks take place.

coercive
Using force or threats to make someone do something.

constitution
The system of beliefs and laws by which a country, state, or organization is governed.

declaration
A document that contains an official statement.

delegate
A person who represents others.

export
To send a product to be sold in another country.

foe
An enemy.

parliament
The group of people who are responsible for making the laws in some kinds of government.

ratify
To give official approval.

repeal
To officially make no longer valid.

tax
An amount of money added to the cost of a good, service, or transaction that is used to pay for things done by the government.

treaty
An official agreement between two or more countries or groups.

For More Information

Books

Marciniak, Kristin. *12 Incredible Facts about the Boston Tea Party.* Mankato, MN: Black Rabbit Books, 2025.

Newell, Chris. *If You Lived During the American Revolution.* New York: Scholastic, 2025.

Shea, Therese. *Women in the American Revolution.* Buffalo, NY: Cavendish Square Publishing, 2025.

Websites

Answers to Questions Kids Ask About the Revolutionary War
www.battlefields.org/learn/articles/answers-questions-kids-ask-about-revolutionary-war

Participation in the American Revolution
education.nationalgeographic.org/resource/participation-american-revolution/

Timeline of the American Revolution
timeline.amrevmuseum.org/intro

About the Author

Marne Ventura is a children's book author and a former elementary school teacher. She holds a master's degree in education with an emphasis in reading and language development from the University of California.

Index

TOP RANK is published by Black Rabbit Books, P.O. Box 227, Mankato, MN, 56002.

• Designed by Danny Nanos • Photographs © Alamy Stock Photo/ Historica Graphica Collection/Heritage Images, 13, North Wind Picture Archives, 25; Associated Press/North Wind Picture Archives, 8-9; Dreamstime/Georgios Kollidas, 35, Nathan Foley, 2, Yalovik Aliaksei, 17; Getty Images/Bettmann, 7, 44; Library of Congress/ William Pether & Thomas Frye, 11; Shutterstock/Belinda Pretorius, 48, Bill Morson, 14–15, CL-Medien, 16, David Smart, 41, djmilic, 10, Dromara, 5, Jim Vallee, 17, Jolygon, 46–47, MAHATHIR MOHD YASIN, 6, Militarist, 39, Morphart Creation, cover, 1, Olivier Le Queinec, 31, Onur ERSIN, 40, 42–43, Perry Cyr, 16, Rudchenko Liliia, 20, spatuletail, 4, 44, vkilikov, 27; Wikimedia Commons/Benjamin West, 38–39, Captain Albert E. Theberge, NOAA Corps (ret.)., 26, Edward Percy Moran, 23, George Caleb Bingham, 28–29, 45, Henry Hudson Kitson, 18, J. Brown/National Archives at College Park, 35, John Singleton Copley, 21, John Trumbull, 2–3, 21, 36, NYPL, 22, public domain, 37, 45, Thomas Jefferson, 24, 45, William B. T. Trego, 32–33, William Barnes Wollen, 19, 44, William Beechey, 12

Library of Congress Cataloging-in-Publication Data: Names: Ventura, Marne author | Title: The American Revolution: 12 things to know / by Marne Ventura. | Description: Mankato, MN: Top Rank is an imprint of Black Rabbit Books, [2026] | Series: America at war | Includes bibliographical references and index. | Audience term: juvenile | Ages 9–13 | Grades 4–6 | Identifiers: LCCN 2024050091 | ISBN 9781644668528 (paperback) | ISBN 9781644668207 (library binding) | ISBN 9781644668849 (ebook) | Subjects: LCSH: United States—History—Revolution, 1775-1783—Miscellanea—Juvenile literature. | Classification: LCC E209 .V46 2026 | DDC 973.3—dc23/ eng/20241122 | LC record available at https://lccn.loc.gov/2024050091